Rescued
by Angels

Rescued by Angels

**The story of miracles
during the Rwandan genocide**

**by Bishop Alexis Bilindabagabo
with Alan Nichols**

ACORN PRESS

Published in English by Acorn Press Ltd, ABN 50 008 549 540
To be published in Norwegian by Norwegian Church Aid and also in the
Kinyrwanda language.

Office and orders:

> PO Box 282
> Brunswick East, Vic 3057
> AUSTRALIA
> Tel/Fax: (03) 9383 1266
> International Tel/Fax: 61 3 9383 1266

National Library of Australia
Cataloguing-in-Publication Data

Bilindabagabo, Alexis, 1956- .
  Rescued by angels : the story of miracles during the
  Rwandan genocide.

  ISBN 0 908284 39 X.

  1. Bilindabagabo, Alexis, 1956- . 2. Barakabaho Foundation.
  3. Genocide - Rwanda. 4. Bishops - Rwanda - Biography.
  5. Rwanda - History - Civil War, 1994 - Atrocities. I.
  Nichols, Alan, 1937- . II. Title.

270.092

Photos: Alan Nichols, Judy Miles, Lea Davis
Art work with permission of National Association of Trauma Counsellors, Rwanda
Cover design: Andrew Moody, Blackburn South
Text layout and design: Kelvin Young, Preston
Map: Ian Heywood, Canberra
Printed by: Openbook Publishers, Adelaide

CONTENTS

ACKNOWLEDGMENTS

Special thanks are due to Jan Harcourt for typing the manuscript from two tapes recorded in Rwanda, and preparing it for the publisher.

NOTE 1: Chapters One to Five were recorded by Bishop Alexis into a tape-recorder during a long conversation with Alan Nichols, making their style more conversational than written.

NOTE 2: According to the identity cards of 1994, the largest ethnic group in Rwanda were the Hutu (sometimes called Bahutu). The second largest group and the target of the genocide were the Tutsi (also called Batutsi). A very small group are the Twa (also called Batwa). An individual would be called Mututsi or Muhutu.

The people of Rwanda as a whole are called Rwandans in English, and Rwandese in French. Bishop Alexis follows the second usage.

Map of Rwanda

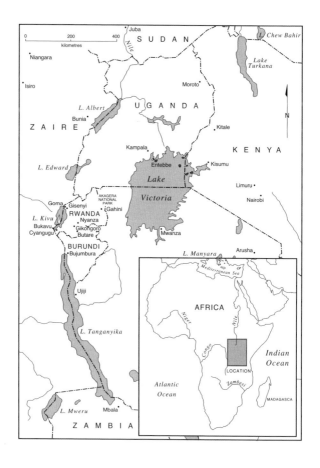

'We walked now into the unknown. We were taken to the commune office, that is the nearest administration post, and the feeling I had was of the loss of a sense of belongingness. You belong nowhere. You are just there. The sense of uprootedness invades you. Ahead of you is nothing. You had parents, you had a school, you had everything to see you through secondary school and university - now you have lost everything, including your parents, your land, your sense of belonging, your everything - now you are just there by yourself. Luckily I had my brother, but now there were only the two of us. And before us was the unknown.'

Bishop Alexis, on the second time he left Rwanda as a refugee.

Prologue
Alan Nichols

I first saw Bishop Alexis on a small plane while flying into Bukavu in Zaire (now called Congo) during the 1994 Rwandan genocide. At the time I was working for World Vision, having spent two years on the Thailand-Burma border working with refugees driven out by the Burmese military regime. I had visited refugees in Jordan, Israel-Palestine, Pakistan-Afghanistan, and many other places, but none of this prepared me for a full-scale genocide and for the sheer terror and panic of hundreds of thousands of people belonging to the minority ethnic group, running for their lives at great risk into neighbouring countries. I was asked by the World Vision Executive team to go to Bukavu because Australian missionary friends, David and Prue Boyd were there with the Church Missionary Society. David was on a ten year assignment to create theological education by extension for clergy in isolated parts, but soon had to turn his hand to caring for five thousand Anglican refugees who arrived on his doorstep. They became part of a much wider team of international and local people caring for six hundred thousand Rwandan refugees who poured across a small bridge at the southern tip of Lake Kivu from Rwanda.

On the aircraft, Bishop Alexis was really obvious because he was wearing a purple stock and clerical collar, so naturally I asked him who he was and where he was going. In simple terms he told me that he had been driven out of Rwanda into Bukavu a month before, but had managed to get his family from there to safety in Nairobi, the capital of Kenya. He was now returning to fulfil a mission that God had given him. 'What was it?' I asked. 'I had a vision from God that I was to be father to the fatherless of Rwanda – to care for all the orphans from this genocide.'

He had absolutely no idea of how to go about this, except for starting with a few people who he knew were already caring for isolated small children found in different parts of Rwanda, who did not appear to have any adults to care for them. Apart from that, he had no idea what being 'father to the fatherless' might mean, but he did know that it meant leaving the church's episcopal leadership for the time being. He would need to create some sort of organisation that would care for children without parents, somehow setting them up in security back in their villages in Rwanda. It was a mammoth idea, given the circumstances and the chaos of the time.

I went into Bukavu with Alexis and stayed with the

Boyd family while Bishop Alexis continued with his, humanly speaking, impossible mission. Meanwhile, there were other Anglican Bishops who had fled with hundreds of their people from all over the country across Rwanda and into the Congo.

This chance encounter on the plane was the beginning of a strong and lasting friendship, and it was also the beginning of a great organisation, the Barakabaho Foundation. But at that moment the Foundation was just a small white cloud on a distant horizon.

I spent several weeks in Bukavu sorting out what to recommend to World Vision Australia about their contribution to the crisis in the Congo. Most of the world focus at the time was on Goma, at the northern end of Lake Kivu, just over the border. This was where the refugees were stopped, unfortunately on most inhospitable country, solid lava rock from nearby volcanoes. Malnutrition, disease, violence, and in the end cholera, wiped out more than fifty thousand of the one million or so people who camped on these unwelcoming slopes.

South in Bukavu, no one died for that reason, but the international agencies and the local Congolese authorities were panicking. They were attempting to get these six hundred thousand refugees through and out of what had

Red Cross Camp 1995, children separated from their parents

been a delightful holiday town on the edge of the lake, and into organised refugee camps. There the supply of food, water, blankets and the necessities of life could be organised properly and shared equitably.

At the end of that time, I recommended to World Vision that their part in the whole disaster might be to offer logistics help, by flying in four wheel drive trucks and large quantities of the supplies required to take on this task.

While I was there doing that, Bishop Alexis was going around trying to understand what was going on with the surviving orphans, and how best to help them. He knew there would be many children, including children under the age of one, in total trauma from the experience they had been through. They would be unable to articulate what they had been through, nor able to get counselling. Alexis felt it was for these children that he had been called, but how to do it would take a long while to work out.

One of his early thoughts was to start small institutions, where forty to fifty children could be cared for at the same time, in a kind of orphanage. Even though there were a few orphanages in Rwanda, the idea was nevertheless alien to Rwandan culture. Before the 1950s, Rwanda had never seen such child care, since in the case of individual tragedies or disasters, children were always taken in by some member of their extended family – aunts, uncles, grandparents. He immediately realised that orphanages were against the culture, and might have the effect of institutionalising these children for years, thus changing the whole nature of their education and upbringing.

His second thought was much more progressive and effective: to start an organisation which would foster children in homes in the villages from where they came, and if possible, with any remaining relatives from anywhere in their extended families. This genesis of an idea was far more progressive than the solution adopted

Returned refugee children back in school in Gahini

by the International non-Government Organisations which did start up orphanages to speed up the process of caring for children. Five years later they were still running these orphanages with the children dressed in distinctive uniforms – something very much against the culture of Central Africa.

By January 1995 Bishop Alexis had registered his new charity organisation, the Barakabaho Foundation, with the Rwandan government, formed out of the Rwandan Patriotic Front, together with political party leaders found in Rwanda. The word Barakabaho means 'let them live', coming from the words often cried out by parents when militia came hunting down their children during the period of April to June, 1994. Parents sent their children into the bush outside their villages, hid them under furniture or tried to carry them to safety – but in the end there were many, many children among the one million Tutsi people killed during this terrible time. 'Let them live' was a cry from the heart, and every Rwandan today knows that the Barakabaho Foundation stands for rescuing children, placing them in alternative families, and giving them a chance for 'life'. The Bible text used was John 10:10, from the words of Jesus found there, 'I am come that they might have life and have it more abundantly.'

More will be said about the Barakabaho Foundation in the Epilogue, since it is the continuing story of Bishop Alexis and his rescue from death.

My own relationship with Rwanda continued from that first visit. In 1995, I was invited by the Archbishops of Melbourne and Canterbury, along with Archdeacon Philip Newman also of Melbourne, to go to Rwanda as guests of the Anglican Church. We were to review the state the Church was in and to see how it was recovering in the aftermath of the genocide, as it appeared that some of its leaders had collaborated with those who organised the genocide. We were also to suggest what might be solutions with regard to future leadership, for at the time there was a problem, as some Bishops, including the then Archbishop, were still outside the country. In some cases, Bishops were accused of not doing enough, or of not warning people in advance of what might happen, when the propaganda was building up prior to April 1994. In other cases they were accused of being 'members' of the radio station which provided both the propaganda in advance of the genocide and also the signal for the attacks to begin on April 6, 1994. Some of these Bishops had fled into exile and six years later have still not returned. Others fled for their lives along with their congregations, but returned as soon as it was possible and took up their office again.

After our visit of 1995, investigations by other representatives from Canada and the UK, and finally a personal visit by the Archbishop of Canterbury to Kenya and Rwanda, the Bishops still in exile were persuaded to resign, so that their successors could be appointed. The upshot was that the Church of Rwanda increased from eight Dioceses (units of church administration led by a Bishop) to nine and there was in the end a team of eleven in a mixed team of Bishops. Prior to that moment, Bishop Alexis had been the only Tutsi elected as a Bishop in the Church. Then the House of Bishops (that is, the Diocesan Bishops all meeting together) de-selected him, making him an Assistant Bishop of the same Diocese. Someone else was appointed Diocesan Bishop and this greatly increased the resentment of the Tutsi within the Anglican Church, as they came to believe that the Church was racially biased against the Tutsi people. So when accusations started flying around in 1994 that the Archbishop and others were involved in the genocide, people believed this only too easily. There has been no evidence of any actual acts of violence against other people or any direct encouragement of killings by these Bishops, but great suspicions remain about their close collaboration with the government of the day which had authorised the genocide, and their silence while it was occurring. The propaganda of 'one nation, one people' was very powerful indeed among the leadership elites of Rwanda.

From 1995, until I had the opportunity of revisiting Rwanda in January 2000 as a consultant to AngliCORD, the Anglican Church gradually reorganised itself. It adopted a new constitution, elected a new Archbishop, Emmanuel Kolini, a Rwandan who had been Bishop of Shaba in Zaire, and from July 1997 operated on a new basis with new Dioceses and new Bishops. Peace was coming within the Church.

This third visit was to conduct a three day workshop on capacity building (developing skills so a local agency can be self-managing and self-sufficient) for the Barakabaho Foundation, the agency Bishop Alexis founded in 1995. The Church was thriving, morale was good, and even in the new Diocesan unit of Gahini where Bishop Alexis is the Diocesan Bishop, there was a great deal of activity, effective outreach, and new organisation. AngliCORD, a national relief and development agency in Australia based in Melbourne, continued right through this period to be a source of funding. The $5,000 given to Bishop Alexis in late 1994 from AngliCORD was the very first seeding grant and it was used to commence the foster care work. Since then, apart from relief funds to the refugees when they were in exile and when they returned home, funds have been given more to development programs. The workshop I conducted with two friends from Melbourne in January 2000, was funded by the Australian Government through AusAid, as part of a two year capacity building program. Rwandans are extremely grateful for this continuing Australian interest.

This background explains how and why I became involved and stayed involved with the Rwandan Church, and with Bishop Alexis personally. One of the projects of the January 2000 visit was to assist him to write a book about his miracle rescues during the genocide. Much interest had been expressed in his story, especially as the

Anglican World, the magazine of the worldwide Anglican communion, quoted a rumour in its June 1994 edition that circulated right round the missionary world, that he had been killed during the genocide. A Church Missionary Society video produced in Bukavu broke the news that he was still alive, and in his travels to support bases in England, Australia and other places, there has been a great deal of interest in his story. Now he tells it in his own words.

CHAPTER 1

Three times a refugee

I was born in a small village around 13 kilometres from Butare in the south of the country. My parents were small-scale farmers with some livestock. I enjoyed milk and grew up strong, enjoying life as a result of being brought up by loving parents. I was the second in a family of five with two sisters and two brothers. I attended the primary school in three places: first near my home, then about five kilometres away and later ten kilometres away. I then went to secondary school, a private secondary school because we didn't have access to public secondary schools because of the ethnic discrimination that was taking place.

In my lifetime I have been a refugee three times. In 1960 there were some political upheavals and our family had to run away because people, mainly of Tutsi origins, were being persecuted. Their houses were burnt down, their cows and goats were eaten and their properties confiscated. Those not killed had to run away for safety. This was the beginning of a long period of agony that lasted over thirty years from when the genocide was launched, and did not stop until July 1994.

Rwandan boy caring for livestock

A refugee child

In 1960, I would have been a boy of around five, as I was born in 1955 and I can still remember some things. In my mind I have an image of houses burning burnt and cows being eaten. I recall people fighting, a group of people coming from one end of the village and another coming from the other end. Later on I discovered that all the people called the Tutsi had their houses burnt and their cows eaten and had to run away.

As a refugee, when you have to run away, you go to

the nearest border crossing spot where you think you can find safety. My father took us all the way to Burundi, as he knew the way there, for in addition to being a small-scale farmer he sold cows in Burundi. When we reached the border he said, 'Let me go back. You cross and I will go back to see what is going on. I'll follow the matter closely and when I think things have cooled down, I'll come back to you.' So we went on and when we reached the border, there was a big river. I remember after we crossed I cried and cried and said, 'Mummy, I can't walk any more!' By that time my mother was tired as she was pregnant and she couldn't carry me. So one of my family, either my older sister or my aunt, just put me on her shoulder in addition to the few belongings she had been able to take. So I was carried as one of the belongings. I'll never forget that experience of crying, 'I just can't make it.' Whenever I think about that day, I think about those people who have to carry children and belongings, then find they have to throw away some of their belongings just so that they can carry the children who aren't able to make it on their own.

This was the beginning of a long and tortuous journey into the unknown for some Rwandese, a journey on which very many perished, for wherever they crossed in Burundi, the Burundians set up roadblocks. Wherever we arrived, we would be told that we must pay some fine. I recall lining up and people saying, 'You know you're not allowed past,' and we would be obliged to pay some fine. This brings back memories of how vulnerable refugees are, because you pay even when you don't know why you should. We paid money and then we would be allowed to go on. We didn't go far from the border, probably just five to ten kilometres inside Burundi, because I remember the refugees used to come to the border to buy potatoes, sweet potatoes and other items. I remember my mother saying that the same person who sold her the potatoes had brought them from her parents' garden. She recognised the sweet potatoes and also the person selling them, for he used to be their neighbour. Imagine buying your own potatoes when you are of refugee status and somebody crosses the border to sell you your own items. And even though some people recognised that it was their own things that were being sold, they had no alternative – they had to buy them anyway, as it was a matter of life and death, an issue of survival.

After some months, I'm not sure how many, my father came back. It was probably six months or thereabouts. I recall that my father came and said, 'Now it is a bit more peaceful, I think we can go home.' So after staying in Burundi for a few months, we went home again. Our house, for some reason I can no longer remember, was not burnt down. Things were stolen but only a few of our cows had been eaten because my father went back and negotiated something, so a few things were salvaged.

Refugee teenagers

Now the period of social revolution in 1973 was a different matter altogether as the group targeted was secondary school students. With regard to the political situation, Habiyarama was Chief of the Armed Forces at that time. He wanted to overthrow the government, and later on, it was he who organised the genocide. To overthrow a government, you need a pretext. How do you find one? It is very simple, you do it by creating chaos. You make the Batutsi scapegoats, then create problems and set up one group against another. You create the problems in schools. People came there and campaigned. I remember one senior government minister coming and he took a group of Bahutu students aside. Later on we could guess what he had shared with them because that very night this group started beating us up, beating up all the Batutsi. We heard that similar things had taken place that week in some other schools and realised the connection with the minister's visit – the Bahutu students had been instructed to beat up all the

Tutsis. Later this same man Habiyarama became president and initiated the genocide of 1994.

We ran away at night and spent the nights outside. When we came back, we found our suitcases had been thrown out. Members of the group said, 'You are just vipers, you shouldn't be here. We'll kill you.' So then we ran away. It was a strange experience to find that somebody who was your friend, a person with whom you had shared everything, should all of a sudden change because he'd been instructed by somebody that this person was an enemy, a serpent, a viper and so he should kill you. This operation of calling people serpents or vipers goes very deep. It tells a person that whenever you see a serpent, your immediate reaction should be to kill the serpent. The terminology used goes deep. You don't have to ask for permission to do this.

All of a sudden things changed for us. Imagine you are studying at school without any problems, then all of a sudden are told that you are not wanted and are now declared a *persona non grata*. Your movements are restricted and discrimination against you is encouraged. Then you are told you don't deserve to live and should quit school, and if you don't, you will find yourself in big trouble. Now this was a private school which we were obliged to attend simply because we were not allowed entry to government schools. These private schools were very expensive and our parents had a lot of difficulty in raising the money, and then after paying for our studies, we were kicked out without even being allowed to sit for our exams.

Now the big question was how to leave the school and reach home safely, a distance of roughly 80 kilometres. Even if I went by taxi, I was not sure whether or not I would be killed in the taxi. But I had to take the risk, because walking on foot was even more risky. After taking a taxi, I then had to walk the last 13 kilometres from Butare to my home village. At one point I imagined that the ground was running away from my feet, and whenever people looked at me, I thought that they wanted to kill me, for that was what I had been told.

On reaching home I found my brother there also. He was in another secondary school and he too had been chased. So when we met at home the big question was, what should we do next? The people being targeted were those in jobs and secondary schools, so our father gave us some money and said, 'I think you'd better try to make it to Burundi again.'

So began my second time as a refugee. We waited until about midnight, making sure that nobody saw us. We had to walk through the bush for almost six hours to reach a cousin living near the border before daylight. We reached there at roughly five in the morning and had to hide for the whole day to make sure that nobody knew we were around. Even though he was our cousin, it was very dangerous for him to hide us, for we were unwanted fellows. He knew how to cross the river – it is a big river – and he knew how to swim it, which parts were shallow, how to deal with crocodiles and everything else. We went at night. My cousin made sure that by four o'clock in the morning, when everybody was deeply asleep, we had crossed the river into Burundi. We were now in a foreign land at night, away from our family, not knowing anybody and without knowing whether or not our family would be killed, leaving just the two of us. We tried to climb a steep mountain near the border and to reach the top, because we didn't want anybody to find us near the shore of the river. I remember my brother and I looking at our identity cards, then tearing them into pieces and saying, 'Goodbye Rwanda, I'll never see you again.'

So we walked now into the unknown. We were taken to the commune office, that is the nearest administration post, and the feeling I had was of the loss of a sense of belongingness. You belong nowhere. You are just there. The sense of uprootedness invades you. Ahead of you is nothing. You had parents, you had a school, you had everything to see you through secondary school and university – now you have lost everything, including your parents, your land, your sense of belonging, your everything – now you are just there by yourself. Luckily I had my brother, but now there were only the two of us. And before us was the unknown. You have no identity, or rather, you have a new identity. You are a 'refused' and you are called a refugee.

The waves subsided after a couple of months and I managed to sneak back to see my parents after the government was overthrown. The person who had lit the fire now quenched it and said that he had obtained peace. My parents were at peace, or rather in pieces, and still at home with our younger brothers and sisters. But because there was no chance of being reinstated in school in Rwanda, I had to go back again to Burundi to look for a school to do my secondary education. I also had to look for my older brother Celestin, the one with whom I escaped, because we had lost each other along the way in Burundi. When I found my way back to Rwanda to see if he had come back home, he wasn't there, so I went back again to look for him. Eventually I found him.

So as a young man of eighteen, I had lost everything and had a sense of hopelessness and one longing only – to obtain a gun. I wanted to buy a gun with the first money I got in my hands on so I could take revenge, that is what I cherished most. And if there were to be a war, I would be amongst the people ready to be recruited, to get revenge. And I was not the only one. Many of us were thinking that way, because when you lose everything and are uprooted, you want to fight everybody.

Nobody seemed to care about me, so I cared about nothing and nobody. I felt the world was against me and I wanted to fight the whole world. And many young people joined the war because they felt they had no alternative, for when you feel mistreated and rejected by society, you feel you are dead, or dying slowly but surely. The temptation is to say, 'better to die with a gun in your hands than to die like a dog.' So fighting becomes a joy rather than a threat. This is partly why there are endless wars in Africa.

The call to ministry

I continued my secondary education in Burundi and returned to Rwanda in 1977. And in August of that year, something special happened to me – that was when I committed my life to Jesus, when I became a born-again Christian. Initially, I had been baptised wholesale into the Roman Catholic church when I was in primary school, but immediately after I left the church, because it didn't mean anything to me. When I became a born-again Christian, I joined the Anglican church because it was the nearest church to me where the Gospel was preached.

Shortly after, I found myself helping the pastor, mainly because I enjoyed teaching the Sunday School. And then, in 1978, I heard the call to the ordained ministry in a rather funny way. As a newly converted Christian, I was very critical of the clergy. But all of a sudden I heard a voice telling me, 'Alex, you have no right to criticise these people unless you join them and become one of them and live as they live, and then in that case you can challenge them.'

I went to the Bishop and the Bishop was willing to recommend me. Initially, I was to go to Uganda to Mukono Theological College, but due to the problems in Uganda it was not possible to go there. Then the Bishop sent me to St Paul's Theological College at Limuru in Kenya and I believe this was really God's working. Arriving at St Paul's at the beginning of 1979, I realised it was a very good theological college for not only were you taught theology, but there was a good input in terms of leadership and training. In my second year as a theological student, I was put in charge of organising games and this proved very successful. In my last year of 1982/3, I became the leader of the senior students, Chairman of the Student Council and learned a lot about leadership and was strengthened in my leadership capacity.

In St Paul's I had received a Bachelor of Divinity with Honours, which was quite good. My favourite subjects were Systematic Theology and Philosophy.

Return to Rwanda

When I came back to Rwanda I began working in the Diocese of Butare for a few months and later on was sent to Bukavu for a six months course in rural development, at the beginning of 1984. That also was very enriching and later on it helped me in my ministry. I then came back to Rwanda to the same Diocese and in 1985 I was ordained Deacon in the Diocese of Butare. In 1986 something special happened to me again, which was to be a great blessing – I married Dr Grace, a medical doctor who had just graduated.

Meanwhile, I was in charge of the planning and development office in the Diocese and that helped shape my character because I had to learn to think independently and to plan, organise and do all sorts of things in the area of creativity. Shortly after my marriage with Dr Grace, I was ordained Pastor, that is, I was priested and given the post of Diocesan Youth Officer. We then shifted and I became a chaplain for a year. I would like to highlight something here. After spending three years as Project Officer, we felt for several reasons that God was calling me to something different. This would mean leaving Butare for a new posting. There was every likelihood that this would take me to a place called Kigeme, for the Diocesan hospital was there and my wife was a medical doctor. I hated Kigeme. I hated that place so much and can remember praying and asking God, 'God, even if you want me to go to that place, please change it because I don't want to go there.'

Ministry in Nyanza

I want to highlight this because later on that was where God called us to go. We didn't go for another four years but instead went to another place, Nyanza. And six years later, Kigeme proved to be the very place where God was to protect us. Our God is really patient. This was God's working. When I went there, I began by being a chaplain for a year and then I was the Dean of Studies in an Anglican secondary school, where I felt I was a fish out of water. The going was really tough and it came to a point where I even resigned from the Diocese. I felt that a lot of things were not right. After many meetings, much prayer and heart searching, I felt persuaded to withdraw my resignation for the sake of the church. Nevertheless, I felt convinced that my call was to the parish and I shared this with my Bishop.

Despite long discussions, the church was very reluctant to send me to be a parish priest because parish priests received virtually no salary. And the Bishop kept saying to me that with your education and your status you will not be able to be paid by the parish. But I told him, 'I'm not looking for money, for I know where I can obtain money.' To go back a bit, I was business-minded and would have done quite well in business. I told him, 'I've come here to serve God, with or without money, I don't mind, but I want to go to the parish.' So I went to the parish and after two years and three months in that parish, it began to shoot up. There was tremendous growth and by the time I left, we had over 1300 active youth in the parish and a parish with over 3000 parishioners, most of them committed Christians.

Missionary Bishop in Cyangugu

Because of the tremendous growth there, when a missionary diocese in Cyangugu was being created and church leaders were looking for a missionary bishop to go down there, I was head and shoulders above everyone else, which is why I was voted overwhelmingly to go to that Diocese.

I was Archdeacon for three months and then elected

Bishop for this newly-created missionary Diocese of Cyangugu. There were a lot of hardships and challenges, but before I continue, I should tell you a bit about my ministry there as a Bishop, and the various changes which took place. After six months as the Bishop of Cyangugu Diocese I found there were a lot of problems and politics in the church there. Some people were very unhappy about me being a Bishop, because of my ethnicity, which was more or less an anathema to them. I could sense it. So after six months of upheavals, problems and the like, I felt God was convincing me that my being a Diocesan Bishop was a stumbling block to many people. Indeed it was a thorn in the flesh of the then politicians, whose cherished idol was ethnic discrimination. In the course of discussion, my position was changed and I was sent to a new Diocese, to Kigeme Diocese, as a Diocesan Bishop. And after six days there I felt God telling me, 'Alexis, there's much more important things to be done than to be a Diocesan Bishop at this particular time. Furthermore, if you insist on staying in that position, you'll not survive for long.'

Assistant Bishop in Kigeme

So I declined to remain as Bishop and offered to become Assistant Bishop to Bishop Norman who at the time was my assistant. I told him, 'You take the seat and then I can become your assistant. And in the meanwhile I'll organise the ministry of evangelisation.' So I remained there as Assistant Bishop, not as a leader, and there were no more problems because I wasn't at the head of the Diocese. I think those who were opposed to my being in that position were now happy. Anyway, I was happy in myself because I could concentrate much more on spiritual programs.

So, that's when I started a new ministry, an organisation dealing with evangelisation, counselling and reconciliation. Initially the ministry was called IDEM (Inter-Diocesan Evangelisation Movement) but before long, some of the bishops who had endorsed it became opposed to it. I could not understand this but it drove me to look for members and I registered the ministry independently of the Anglican Church and with a new name. That organisation today is doing wonderful work in evangelisation and reconciliation in the country. The charity is called MOUCECORE (in French, 'Movement Chrétien pour l'évangelisation, le councelling et la réconciliation'). Praise God, because this ministry is now appreciated by all the Dioceses, and indeed all the Christian churches in Rwanda.

When I shifted, I went immediately to Kigeme, and that's where we stayed all through the time that the genocide was being preached. Some killings were already taking place here and there and I am sure that if I had been a Diocesan Bishop then I would have been killed in that particular period. I would not have lasted until the actual genocide. I remained there until the time of the genocide and lived through it for three months, until I moved out with my family.

I would then become a refugee in Bukavu for the third time, this time crossing as a Bishop – the first time I was taken by my parents, the second time, I took myself, and the third time I took my wife and four children – going again into the unknown. But the Almighty was with me and everything seemed to be organised for us wherever we went, even our crossing into Bukavu. The Bishop there was a friend of mine from the time I lived there when I did my course in rural development. Where I crossed this third time it was to the same place, so I had many friends there, or rather brothers and sisters in the Lord. We were given a very good house, a warm welcome and all we really needed, with the possibility of linking up with whatever else was yet to come.

Anyway, being a refugee three times in my life has been quite an experience but I long not to have to become a refugee for a fourth time, for that would be too much for me to bear.

CHAPTER TWO

Origins of a genocide

You cannot talk about events leading to the genocide without looking at it from the beginning. The Rwandese used to live together harmoniously at some levels. Before the coming of the Belgians as a colonial power, you never saw people really fighting along ethnic lines with the Bahutu, the Batutsi and the Batwa, setting one group against the other. They were beginning to merge into socio-economic classes, with 'haves' and 'have nots'. The 'haves' were the Batutsi, those with many cows and the 'have nots', called the Bahutu. were agriculturalists. At the lower strata of society were the Batwa, the forest hunters. Through intermarriage, all these groups were beginning to merge into one, but when the Belgians came, the process of divide and rule was set in motion as the line of divide became clearly drawn.

Belgian colonisation

Back in the 1930s, the Belgians introduced identity cards. These fixed people into the various ethnic groups once and for all. If your father's identity card at this time stated his ethnic status was a Mututsi, that fixed your identity permanently, no matter that you crossed the ethnic divide if you married a Muhutu wife, no matter how many cows you had. Before these lines were clearly drawn, it was very difficult to tell who was who. Now it became very easy – if you had more than ten cows you were simply called Batutsi – Batutsi had become more a social and economic class than an ethnic group.

If you take my community of Rwanda, you come up with a similar scenario to anywhere else, with the cream of society (the rich) in the minority and the middle class in the majority. A few are found in the lowest strata – the downtrodden and the forgotten – as in every society. This explains why even today, the Batwa are not talked of, as they are in this category. What is peculiar to Rwanda is that the Rwandese community is made up of three distinct ethnic groups, nobody knows why, and that over time, these three merged into one group.

When the lines of identity were fixed, any Bahutu with more than ten cows became known as Batutsi and those without cows were divided into the Bahutu or the Batwa. This created an awkward situation, for before the 1940s, those taking part in leadership as chiefs throughout the country were drawn from all three ethnic origins, but now their Belgian colonial masters systematically demoted them and fixed only the Batutsi as leaders.

The introduction of an elite group angered the other groups a lot and rather than the colonial master being seen as the exploiter, this fell to the Batutsi who had to execute the master's orders. Whipping was introduced along with everything else, but rather than anger falling on the Belgians, all the mistakes made by the colonial masters were put on the Batutsi. In the 1950s, the educated elite among the Tutsis started seeking independence for the country. Belgium wouldn't accept this and decided to change sides. They then began to forge the population figures to make it look as if the Hutus were in the majority so they could say 'We are supporting the majority tribe now.'

From then on, Belgium claimed that the Bahutu made up 90 per cent, the Batutsi nine per cent and the Batwa one per cent of the population. After they killed many Batutsi in the 1960s, the statistics remained the same and today, even after one million Tutsis were killed in 1994, if you ask anybody what percentage of the population they make up, they still tell you the same figures. It has become 'gospel' truth. All through these years we had to recite that the Hutus made up 90 per cent of the population, the Tutsis nine per cent and the Batwas one per cent. So as they were in the majority, the Hutus had the most rights. It was only after the genocide that

I discovered that this continuous repetition of false population figures was hiding the actual numbers of a given portion of the population. It allowed you to kill them slowly, to gradually finish them off. Then you could say, 'They never existed – we have the figures to prove it.' It was a way of getting rid of unwanted persons as figures could be manipulated. And in the years between 1960 and 1994, just being called Mututsi was enough for a person to deserve jail or death, you did not have to commit any other crime.

The seeds of genocide

The seeds of genocide were planted in the 1930s and watered. It was like putting manure on the garden and watering the seeds. I would say that the first attempt at genocide was made in the 1960s, when the first lot began to be killed and some ran away. The leaders started teaching people a distorted history, portraying the Tutsis as imposters and calling them all sorts of names. You can find evidence for this in various books and see how these ideas were presented.

Two particular things were to play a big role during the genocide. One was the notion that a Mututsi was a snake, and in Rwandese mentality, when you see a snake you have to kill it – you can't let it escape, even if it goes inside the house. And if it goes inside a precious thing, you must break it and kill that snake, because it is the number one enemy of human beings. So when a person is portrayed as a snake, you predispose people, create the idea in their mind, that whenever they see a snake, they must kill it.

The second notion was the distorting of our history, saying that the Tutsis were outsiders who had originally come from Ethiopia. That is why people like Mugesera and others said that they had to send the Batutsi back to where they belonged, and they could take a short cut by throwing the people into the river. As the river ran into Nile near Ethiopia the Tutsis could then flow back to where they belonged in Ethiopia.

But to arrive at these two ideas, history had to be distorted. Psychological torture then started. I was at school then and like many children branded Batutsi, we would be instructed to stand up and then told, 'Batutsis, put your hands up.' It was very frustrating and you felt that you were a second-class citizen. If you do the statistics, you will soon discover that all Batutsi children who lived in Rwanda after 1960 hate history. We hated it because we were told that we were a bad ethnic group. Whenever it was the time for history, we felt like running away and coming back after the lesson finished. They kept referring to our grandfathers as exploiters, as bad people, and all sorts of other silly things. History was distorted and the very people who learned history as children during the 1960s and who grew up in that atmosphere, were those who later implemented the genocide.

Deep down in our hearts we knew that what we were being taught was wrong, and when I grew up, I asked my father the truth about this. He told me that it was not true and that neither he, nor his father, nor even his grandfather had wronged anyone. Yes, they had their cows but they had exploited or wronged no one. They were Rwandese and had heard of no other origin for Tutsis apart from belonging to Rwanda. Many families had a similar story.

Ethnic discrimination in education

In 1973, many Hutu secondary school children were allowed to continue through school even though they were failing their courses, while many Tutsi students who were doing very well were kicked out. This was the result of government policies that favoured Hutus, so those who failed continued at school. One fellow I know was failing miserably in all subjects at school. Later on I met him and found he was an officer in the army, meaning that he had gone through secondary school. If half of a class is expelled, then the other half has to be carried forward. So fellows brought up and protected by the system continued their studies in a bad system, learning that the solution to any problem was to kill, chase or to expel the Batutsi, because they would always get something out of it.

These fellows then went to university. The system was organised in such a way that they had to be pushed along even though they were not doing well, meaning that the system of education was distorted to favour some of them. Later on they were given degrees or other qualifications they didn't deserve and obtained high positions as directors of institutions and the like, but in reality, they couldn't make it educationally. This meant that in 1990 or shortly before, serious economic problems arose in the country. People began talking about various problems here and there and became discontented, so a solution to the situation had to be found. The then president, Habiyarama, managed to lie to the international community, saying that Rwanda was the most peaceful country in the world. And everybody believed that! We used to hear the slogan, 'We don't have gold and we don't have diamond, but our gold and our diamond is peace.' Everybody repeated it. But beneath that so-called peace was ethnic discrimination, corruption and all sorts of evil, but still the whole world believed him.

Civil War

Now a big issue began to arise in the 1980s and through into the 1990s. The refugees who had run away from the country in the 1960s and1970s began to say, 'If you say that Rwanda is peaceful, why don't you allow us to come back?' And Habiyarama would say, 'But Rwanda is very, very small.' The refugees would say in reply, 'We are not looking for land, we are not looking for anything, we can find a way. We can look for jobs, we can set up businesses, we can buy, we can do this or that, all we need is to be given the right to come back to our motherland.' And he would say, 'No, we can't fit you in – it's just too small. It's like a full cup. Any drop would just make it overflow.' And so the refugees began to say, 'If you don't allow us to come peacefully, we shall come forcibly'. In whatever country they were, they had been made to feel second-class citizens. They knew that they were not wanted, they were foreigners but having now fought in various armies of other countries, they said, 'If you won't allow us to come back peacefully, we'll have no choice but to come back and fight.'

The war started on the first of October in 1990. On the fourth, less than three days later, the government devised a policy to eliminate any so-called collaborators, that is, all those called the Batutsi. The Hutus began to say that the refugees living outside the country were going to attack their relatives, thus making all remaining Tutsis collaborators. In Kigali, some sort of shooting drama was created to demonstrate that there were collaborators even inside Kigali, giving the leaders a pretext for getting hold of anyone they wanted to arrest.

Very many people were thrown into prison but I managed to survive that period. A number of factors protected me or I would have been put in prison. If I had been imprisoned I would probably have died there because of the bad conditions – no bed, no water, overcrowding. Right from the time when intensive teaching about genocide started openly, people were put in prison. Some died straight away, some were killed slowly, while others survived and were released.

How political control was gained

People were trained to become killers using the classic methods: establishing militias, using the media and employing political control. You get a group of people together and have seminars, teaching them day and night, training them mentally and physically to be killers or to supervise the killing. Intensive training was made possible because over a period of three years, money for this purpose was readily available. Some banks gave loans to people, thinking that they were going to set up a business, except the business was to train the militia and later on, to pay the killers. That was the first thing.

The second method used was manipulation through the media. The national radio, there was only one, was used as well as the national television and also a private radio/television, set up purposefully for propaganda use. And this was done very subtly with impressive music. If you look at the message, it was crazy, but everybody loved it. There was talk about the Batutsi and the Bahutu and everything else, with some distorted history as well, all put in a very attractive manner. A good number of journals published terrible articles that inspired ethnic hatred. One famous one was called *Kaguri*. Even the sight of it threatened some people. If you review my sermons right through that period, you will see that I was forever talking about the evil of ethnic discrimination, about how division was evil and about how we are made in God's image etc. I will never forget my sermon at Easter in March 1994, because I was preaching at a big conference organised by Scripture Union, shortly before the genocide. I preached and talked about the evil happenings and how Christians should dissociate themselves from evil, avoid ethnic discrimination and speaking bad words and not create divisions between people and the like.

The intense teaching was supplemented by political control of the whole of society from top to bottom. It reached from the head of state down to the lowest level. With the President at the top, the country was divided into ten prefectures each headed by a prefect. Each prefecture was divided into ten and fifteen communes. The communes were divided into seven or eight sectors, each of these divided into cells and the cells divided into ten houses. With that structure, the whole of society could be controlled. Those supporting the power structure and the ideology of genocide were then put into position to make sure that at whatever meeting held, these elements were put across.

These three methods were used and used most effectively. The majority of the Rwandese population, being without formal education, was to begin with, quite receptive of the leader's word, taking it as gospel truth. No matter what message I preached on a Sunday, government officials contradicted it throughout the week.

During the period from 1990 to 1994, a number of people were killed. The genocide had begun. You would hear of a whole village being killed by unidentified people and the announcer on the radio would say, 'In such and such a village, two hundred people have been killed by unidentified enemies.' This was not true, as the killers were clearly identifiable and the police, the military and everybody else, all of them supported and congratulated them. In the area in Nyanza where I was staying as a pastor, I was told that a group of between thirty and sixty young people would come to a place and ally themselves politically with the people accommodating them. They would stay for a couple of days, going out at night with others from the same area with the same ideology, and they would slaughter people. After that, they would get onto government buses and go home to where they had come from – to Kigali or somewhere in the north. I saw these men too, but fortunately killings did not take place or I would have been among those killed at that particular time.

They found it difficult to find allies among the local population in this area because people denounced them and said openly to them, 'We know why you are here – you have come to kill us.' People would then sleep outside their houses, ready to hide or run away if the killers started to come to do their dirty work.

Genocide started right back in 1991. Reports of people being slaughtered here and there were being sent to the United Nations and other international bodies. Although the genocide was known, no steps were taken against it. Nothing was done. Rwandese were prepared for it for they had learned from the 1960s that if they slaughtered Tutsis they could have their land and so would be rewarded. They stole cows and ate them. Some were able to return to their studies because their colleagues had been chased out. They were rewarded. The government did not have to promise them incentives to do the killing, they already knew that if you killed somebody, you could own his land, it was as simple as that. You kill somebody, you eat his cows, that's it. You kill somebody, you get his position, that's it. So, people were already motivated and said, 'We're looking forward to the time when we can just enjoy it.'

Another element was the economic pressure that was on Rwanda. It was very easy for government leaders to say, 'Look here, if you kill the Tutsis everything will be fine. The problems you have are because of the Tutsis. If you don't have money it's because the Tutsis are taking the money outside the country. If you don't have schools it is because the Tutsis have gone into schools. So get rid of them and everything will be all right. If you don't have jobs, it's because the Tutsis are in the jobs. Get rid of them and everything will be all right.'

Imagine you have a group of jobless young fellows and you tell them that they are jobless because other people are occupying the jobs they should have. Then tell them that these people are foreigners. Because of the way history had been distorted you are now accustomed to being told that these people are foreigners, that they are not Rwandese. So what do you think will happen?

The following is one person's, Jeremy's, confession:

'In 1990, my father-in-law was jailed, so were many of my friends. My parishioners were jailed and I visited them often. Then my Bahutu friends in high government positions warned me that it was too dangerous for me to continue to visit them as they were considering jailing me as well. I did not stay because I knew that only too well. In fact, being in prison or being outside was almost the same to me, with the only difference being that I could help more from outside than inside. My heart was bleeding and I was ready for anything.'

The Bible tells us that our human nature is such that we are inclined to learn bad things very easily, they are driven in very easily. So it was easy to educate the whole population – the message was easy to understand. The genocide started on a small scale and people seemed to be just waiting to be told to start the dirty work.

CHAPTER THREE:
The genocide becomes personal

Kigeme is one of the old missionary stations of the Anglican church in Rwanda. It is built on three small hills that appear rather like three stones. The cathedral and the Diocesan offices are on one of them, on the second are the hospital and a few houses for the hospital staff, and on the third, a secondary school and a few houses for the secondary school teachers. The hills are each separated by about 500 metres and small streets join the three. They are so close to each other that you can see what is happening across on the other hills.

I lived there for two years before the genocide began, as Assistant Bishop assisting Bishop Norman Kayumba. We were there under very difficult financial constraints but were lucky as both Bishop Norman and his wife were committed Christians, so we had a wonderful time together. We never had any head-on collisions on anything, for although we disagreed with each other on a number of things, we never disagreed in public. On the whole, we had a wonderful relationship with him, his wife and his children. Our characters were different but we saw them as complementary, and as a result I enjoyed the work. I enjoyed assisting him because he didn't become a bother, and I think he enjoyed having me because I didn't bother him about anything, including my salary when there wasn't any money. My wife was employed as a government medical doctor, so we did not have to depend on my stipend to live. Having my own vehicle was of great assistance, as the Diocese had only one and Norman used it.

At the beginning we didn't even have an office so I worked either from home or wherever else there was room. There were serious constraints on us but there was also joy in the sense that there was co-operation between us as well as understanding and mutual respect, which was a great help. That was God's provision, giving me such a supportive Bishop, otherwise he might have betrayed me and I would have died during the genocide. This was the very place I had specifically requested the Lord not to send me to four years before, for I hated Kigeme. But God prepared the ground there for my wife and I, and when we were sent there, we went joyfully, ready to serve the Lord. And it is there that the actual genocide of 1994 met me.

The genocide in Kigeme

At the time the genocide started, Bishop Norman was living seven kilometres away from the Diocese centre, in the town of Gikongoro. I as his only assistant, was living in Kigeme. On April 6, 1994 we heard that the presidential plane had been shot down and by the following day, roadblocks were declared everywhere and people had to stay inside. We did not know exactly what was happening but I felt that things were going to be very, very difficult, knowing that tension had already built up.

On the seventh, we heard of the first killing when the corpse of a young man we knew very well was brought to the hospital. Just as we were preparing to go for the burial, we saw many wounded people coming. As they were running, we knew that the killings had started, and very quickly, before the end of the day, we knew who was doing the killing and who was being killed. If you were a Tutsi you were to be killed and the Bahutu were the ones killing the Batutsi.

I must confess here that not all the Bahutu were murdering, contrary to what people think. Killers were organised into groups and came from some distance away. Later on when I discovered that the killings were so systematic, I realised that they had to have started from a particular point, starting from the border to make sure that no one could run away, then moving inwards. This explained why we could see people coming from a distance. Roadblocks were systematically erected to make sure that even those who hid had nowhere to pass. Then they were literally hunted down.

So it was on the seventh, when people started running away from the killing, that we discovered that we were also threatened. Our house was on a small street, close to the road that joined the Cathedral office and the hospital. This increased our risk of being killed so we shifted to the secondary school, not knowing where refugees should go for safety. The secondary school had a big multi-purpose hall that was available during the day so it seemed ideal. We thought it best to tell all the refugees to group in the school rather than to have them scattered anywhere.

Preparing for Heaven

We went to the hall and many people started arriving. By the evening of the seventh or eighth, I don't remember which exactly, there were lots and lots of people, up to three hundred. And when I saw them, I felt that God was telling me, 'You never know, but these people might not have long to live. It is high time for you to prepare them for heaven.' Because I had to take charge of everything, wondering how to feed people and everything else, I did not have time to do this myself as I couldn't stay put in one place. So I requested one dear brother who was there, a pastor named the Reverend Ruhamya Silas, who has since gone to heaven, and told him, 'We don't know how long these people will live, so let's tell them about heaven and how to prepare for heaven.' He did this and started teaching them about how to be reconciled with God and with themselves, that they should not hate anyone nor have a spirit of revenge, and that they should repent and other similar things.

And this group of people took the teachings very seriously. The situation had moved so fast that I knew that people were actually being prepared for heaven. And almost all of these people, and I may not be wrong if I say all of them, all went to heaven. One week later they were all dead. None escaped death.

The first miracle

On the tenth of October, we witnessed the first miracle. The militia had gone around killing people and we could see them burning houses and eating cows. Because Kigeme is situated on the top of hills, we could see across them for long distances and watch what was happening – cows being chopped into pieces, houses burning and thousands of militia streaming from the villages across the hills, after finishing their dirty work. They had come back pretty early. The reason I think they finished quickly was because they were not supposed to kill after dark. The whole thing was coordinated so as to minimise their risks, so they had to kill during the day, know exactly who they had killed and also who had escaped, so that they could hunt them down.

They were organised to kill between eight o'clock in the morning and two in the afternoon, then stop and continue the following day. But this day they came at roughly two or three o'clock and reached the streets across from the school. Someone probably told them there were about three hundred people in the school so why not they go and kill them. They stopped and three of them, probably spies, came to see whether we were armed or protected and where to attack. I watched these three guys from a distance. When they were about 50 metres away, I knew they had not come to help us. I knew they were spies who simply wanted to know if any people were still there or if there was any resistance or fight so that they might be prepared. They came to within a few metres of where I was and hid their weapons – I imagine spears and machetes and the like.

So they met me at the door of the hall and told me, 'Bishop, we are coming to warn you that in a few minutes you'll be killed. The militia are coming to kill you.' I told them, 'There are angels protecting us and surrounding this place. They will not allow you to kill us. And if they do, we know where we are going. We will be going to heaven.' This came out spontaneously just like that, that's the truth. It was an immediate response.

So these three boys went back and after thirty minutes they returned. When they reached a certain spot I heard whistles. This seemed to be how the militia received their commands, with various whistle signals meaning 'attack' or 'retreat' or whatever. They used whistles because there were so many of them there was no way their leaders could shout and make sense. When I heard the whistles I thought it was probably the signal to move in and attack, but instead I saw them going away. They just left.

When some of the people heard we were about to be attacked, they wanted to look for weapons, machetes and spears. I told them that violence was not good and said, 'No, God is protecting us, we don't want to fight. Our weapon is prayer and we have to rely on God's protection, on him alone. We don't want anybody to have weapons, we just want to be in God's hand and God will protect us'. So they threw away any weapons they had.

Later on, after I had time to reflect, I said to myself, 'Why was it that whenever people came to attack us, they never passed that particular spot?' And then I realised that this was the very spot where I had talked to the three boys about angels, where the roads going to the hospital and the school met and the road to the school branched off. Each time people came to attack, no one ever passed that spot. I could remember them saying, 'What are we doing here, why don't we just go home?' and then blowing their whistles and leaving.

So, that was the first miracle. The killers had left the main road on their way to attack us, were half way there and with less than 200 metres to go, stopped, blew their whistles and departed. Why this should happen was inexplicable for if they had kept coming, they would have killed all of us. We would not have fought, so we would have perished.

Government 'protection'

Now came a difficult choice for us. As threats increased, Bishop Norman did not know what to do. He came and I told him about the whole situation and he said to me, 'Let me go and plead with the political authorities to give us protection.' So all the political authorities came – the

Prefect, who was the topmost political leader in the area, the Major, the commander of the police in the area and the Burgomaster, the head of our local commune. Because they all came, I assumed they didn't know what they had in mind to do, so I felt safe enough to venture out with Bishop Norman to the office where they had gathered. They told Norman, 'Bishop we haven't enough soldiers to come and protect groups of people here and there. The only thing we can do is to send a police escort for them because there's no way the people can cover the seven kilometres to Gikongoro (the administrative headquarters) alone. So if we can take them there, we can give them protection together with the other refugees.'

Now when a political leader tells you that, you do not imagine they have any other intentions. Yet for reasons I still cannot tell, I replied, 'I, my family, my wife and children, shall remain here with or without protection, because God has called me to serve him here. If it is time for us to go to heaven, I would rather go to heaven from Kigeme, from the place where God has called me to serve him, than from the Gikongoro.' So I decided that we were staying there. Then the Prefect announced to the refugees, 'Those of you who accept to remain here are free to remain knowing that you have no protection.' We tried to convince some of them to take the risk and remain but only ten Batutsi secondary school students elected to stay behind. They had stayed behind for the holidays in the one remaining class, and these students were the only ones there who survived the genocide.

The others said, 'No, we will go because the political authorities tell us that they will protect us, so we will go to where we can get protection. We cannot remain here without protection.' I stayed on there, knowing that we would be killed within two or three days, four days at the maximum. But seeing what was happening, I was beginning to feel that probably death would be better than life.

So within two or three days, the police were sent, and we saw these people depart. I will never forget this – the children who had played with our children, our co-workers, people who had been diocesan workers, others we knew, friends and relatives – that was the last time we saw those people. I remember my wife grabbing Bibles, Scripture Union booklets, anything she could get hold of, to give to various people, to help them later on. We parted company and one week later, probably on the Wednesday, we learnt that all these people, together with the others there, roughly around ten thousand people, were butchered in Gikongoro, just a few kilometres away from where we were, after a week of starvation. They were slaughtered in the most shameful manner, just a few metres away from where the political leaders who had promised them protection were stationed.

It was a difficult choice to make to stay at the diocesan offices without knowing where it would take us. Looking back, we can see that God was leading us but at the time we did not understand, and simply closed our eyes and followed him in faith.

A litany of suffering

Now followed a litany of suffering. We had left our house and were living at the school in the house of the headmistress. It had a telephone so we could phone out and be reached by telephone. Each time we rang we would be told that 'so and so has been killed together with his family.' 'So and so has been killed with his family.' 'So and so has been killed with his family.' 'Your whole family has been wiped out. No one is still alive in your family.' I heard these stories for one week, then two weeks and then it was too much for me, too much. It went on and on like that. Sometimes I would ring somebody and be told, 'If you ring and there's no reply, then you know what has happened,' meaning, 'you understand.' And I remember ringing a friend and he said, 'They are coming.' That was the last word I heard from him.

Ntarama – genocide museum 1995

From early on I can remember who was being targeted – enemy number one were the Batutsi and orders had been given to wipe them all out. The second group targeted were those Bahutu who had openly opposed the killing. I can remember ringing a good friend of mine in Kigali, a dear brother in the Lord called Israel Hamiginana, who was the leader of the African Evangelistic Enterprise and I learnt that he and his wife and children had all been killed. I remember too my younger brother Ngendahayo Emmanuel, a young businessman living in Nyanza, who was very charming and loved by many people. When he rang me, I told him, 'You are still young, try your luck and trust in God regarding the question of your surviving, even though I don't see how you can.' That was the last time we talked. I never saw him again. He tried to run away but was caught on the way and killed. I don't know where, how or anything else. He was in his late twenties.

It was so painful. I rang the Bishop of Butare and asked him to enquire about my family because they lived only thirteen kilometres away from Butare. He said, 'Ring again in the afternoon, I'll have the news.' And he told me, 'Your father, your mother, your sisters, your cousins, they have been all wiped out. The only one who has disappeared who they don't know where he is, is your older brother, but they are still hunting for him.'

And I didn't know whether I should keep on ringing or not, but in any case, gradually there were no more people left for me to ring, there was nothing else to inquire about because I knew it all. And a big question mark started to grow in my head for I kept wondering, 'Even if I do live, where shall I live, how shall I live, to whom shall I relate?' I mean, I had so many unanswered questions. There I was with my wife and four children when one of my parishioners came to visit us. She was a Muhutu, but had refused to go to other families even though they were telling her, 'If they come to kill the Bishop and his wife and children, they'll kill you as well.' She refused to go and said, 'No, I'll stay here. If they kill them, let them kill us together. I don't mind.' Now she was trapped and couldn't travel. She felt that we were her family and didn't want to abandon us.

So, there we were. The lady who was working for us in the house – the housekeeper – was a Hutu but she continued working. The gardener was a Hutu and he continued his work. We were all trapped. You can imagine what it was like when the whole day you kept hearing all these terrible things, saw houses burning, people being killed or hearing about people being killed. What was even more terrible was how people were being killed, with all sorts of tortures. There were stories of how they would come and peel off your skin and tie you to a tree and leave you for the birds or dogs to come and eat while you were still alive. They would tell you about how they would kill you. They would start with your younger child, then your other children and then lastly they would kill your wife and if you were lucky they would not rape her in front of you. And then you would be killed last. These stories were being told over and over again by people passing and telling these stories and I could hear them because my house was near the path where they passed while I was sitting inside there. And lots and lots of questions kept going round in my head.

The manipulation of statistics

There was this litany of suffering, with these stories being repeated over and over again. One devastating thing I learned was that my whole village, no three-quarters of my whole village, was wiped out systematically. Throughout the country, the scale of killing was so high that if they talk of one million people, it was definitely much more than that. Even now, when I visit many places, I can see with my own eyes that in certain villages at least one house in three was burnt.

Sometimes people are misled by the statistics. I have already told you how they played with the statistics so that they could kill people and later on explain that no people were there, but this was simply because they had killed them. These statistics are quite misleading and I have no doubt that the numbers of people killed during the genocide number over a million. There must be over a million because most of the families were completely wiped out, for instance, as I have already said, in my own village, which is quite big, three-quarters of the population were killed. So it was not a few people, but a lot.

Traumatised

One day I called on a young girl aged sixteen or seventeen years and informed her I had just learnt that her father and mother and brother and sisters had all been wiped out. Her only surviving brother, who was in hiding, communicated this to me. I told her this, fearing that she would break down in tears, but strangely, she didn't shed a tear. I felt she didn't understand, for she just looked at me, then looked down as if saying, 'I was expecting it. I was ready for that.' So my wife and I prayed for her together and she left.

My big dilemma was that staying alive seemed so much more problematic than dying, because if I were to survive the question now was, 'With whom shall I relate, where shall I go, how shall I work?' There were so many unanswered questions such as how shall I cope with what I have heard, all this terrible loss and everything else. Death was probably preferable, better than staying alive, but then the big question was how would I die. And each time I thought about how people were being killed and all the torture and everything else, I felt like shedding tears and felt my heart suffering so much. It was very difficult to accept and cope with it.

Victory over fear

I lived with it for a couple of weeks and it went on and on like that until I felt so traumatised and afraid that I simply had to pray. And I remember my oldest daughter, who was aged six by then, praying with the other children, the secondary school students who were there also with us waiting for death, and she came and shared with us what they were praying for. And I remember something she said that I would call the big challenge, and from out of it came victory. I heard a voice telling me, 'Alex, you have been telling people about heaven, you have been preaching and telling people to be reconciled with God and to be prepared to go to heaven. Now when heaven is knocking at your door, it seems as if you are saying, "No."' So I remember praying and saying, 'Lord, I'm ready. I'm prepared.' And with that came victory – victory over fear and victory over death, because I now felt heaven was pretty near and knocking at my door. Heaven was what I was longing for, even though I didn't know in what way I was going to get there. I can remember meditating a lot on the words of Paul to the Philippians, chapter 1, verse 21, 'For to me, to live is Christ and to die is gain.'

rescued   by   y

CHAPTER FOUR

The greatest miracles

My fear now faded away and great miracles emerged. It is very easy to talk about the peace of God which passes all understanding, which preserves your heart and mind in the knowledge of God, but it is quite different to experience it. This is what happened. You know you are going to be killed anytime, yet you have the peace of God. You do not accept death or become resigned to your fate just because you have no other way out, but because death is a reality and the way to eternal life. And this is what gives you peace.

I started seeing things with different eyes and used to joke with my wife, telling her, 'Let's go to bed. They'll probably kill us when we are asleep and we will go straight to heaven.' I no longer took death to be anything important and even stopped thinking about the 'how', really trusting in God, that God knew and if God meant us to suffer, then we were ready even for suffering. That was a great miracle.

And a second miracle was this, that when you've gone through this litany of suffering, when you have been told your parents have been killed, your relatives have been killed, your friends have been killed, there is the tendency to hate the killers. But I didn't feel this sentiment of hatred or of hating anybody, and instead felt at peace and at ease with myself.

Flowing out of that was a third big miracle. In one sense I did not understand what was taking place but in another, I accepted what was taking place without approving of it. There comes a time when although you do not approve of something, you can accept it. You say, 'God, I don't understand, but you are still God and you are still caring and you are still a father and a loving father, despite what is taking place.'

Even though I saw so many miracles, I would say that these three miracles were the biggest ones, because there is the tendency when you know that you could be killed any time, to lose sleep, to lose your appetite, to even die before your actual death. But it was strange for we were eating and sleeping while knowing they could kill us at any time, and this is victory over death. Even if a medical doctor tells you that you are going to die within a few days, you will probably die before the actual time.

Yet when you know that killers could arrive anytime and you go to bed and sleep like a baby, then that gift can only come from the Almighty. And the same when you find you can eat, that gift can only come from the Almighty, for otherwise, we would have become sick or whatever during the three months we waited for death.

So for me, this was a very crucial and important time, when we felt the reality of heaven and the reality of death as our entry into eternal life, and we accepted it. And we knew too the reality of the peace of God which passes all understanding and which was able to keep our minds and hearts even from hatred, when there was every justifiable reason for hating or wanting to hit back at the killers.

Protected by angels

One man really wanted me dead. He was a Muslim called Abdul and he led one of several groups of militia and organised a series of attacks. Before each attack people would tell me, 'Abdul is coming with his group, they are coming to kill you.' Although I can tell you many stories about him, I'll mention just a few incidents.

A group came to the particular spot I talked about earlier, where I said the angels were stationed to protect us. They stopped there and started discussing something together. On this day, somebody raised the question, 'By the way, have the Roman Catholics killed their Bishops?' and someone else replied, 'No. They haven't yet.' Then another said, 'So why should we kill our Bishop?' and one replied, 'No way, we are not going, we are not moving,' but the others told him, 'Go home, we're not going to kill him now.'

In the other incident, somebody said, 'If you allow people to come and enter the school, they will destroy our school. We have killed all the Batutsi we wanted so why should we allow people to come and destroy our school?' So it was that through the process of protecting the school, they also protected us, as if we were just part of the property. Because the property was being protected, we were protected as well.

Another time somebody said, 'There's only Bishop Alex left so if you kill him we'll never get any more external support. All his friends will know that we have killed him so they won't support us any more.' Obviously they must have known that the people from their district were being helped a lot by the bursar, who was paying for their children's education and that I also helped them. Someone else also said, 'We have killed all the Batutsi but if you kill him, the people outside will no longer help or support us, so let's not kill him.' Their point was that now that they had finished the killing they wanted life to go on unhindered, and so they went away.

Sometimes they would arrive at the spot where I had told them that angels were protecting us, and there would be arguments and then they would part company and go home. Another time there were two people they particularly wanted from the hospital, so Abdul passed by leading the biggest group, and there were several other groups of militia led by different leaders. As leader of the biggest group, Abdul wanted to kill Bishop Alex and his family. There was a pick-up truck at the hospital that he had obviously taken from someone he had killed, because he didn't own one. Now he used to drive it wherever he was told to go, putting in it anything he wanted to steal from victims. At the hospital he found two containers of milk that had been sent by a Swiss agency. I had requested this milk the previous year to help some people from around there who were malnourished and in poor health, but little did I know that God would use this milk to protect me. Abdul wanted that milk so he went back with his pick-up truck to get the containers. He was just about to open them when the people – they were Anglicans, good Anglicans from around there – noticed that he wanted to steal the milk. They became so angry with him and said, 'Now you have been saying that you want Bishop Alex, but apparently what you really want is to destroy our property and to steal our milk. You want to steal our things.' So they took the vehicle and chased him away, telling him never to return. And that was the end of Abdul and his mission to kill Bishop Alex.

Several other attempts were made on us. Each time something reversed the situation and it came to a standstill. Surely the angels of the Lord were present, for how else could we explain how it was that the killers never passed that particular spot, and even those who tried to cross, became as humble and good as any person could be.

The soldiers come for me

All this happened in May. So many people had been killed that only a very few remained and they were in hiding, here and there. Soldiers came enquiring about who had been killed, who remained and the like. Bishop Norman had shifted back from Gikongoro and was living in the house next to mine, so I saw the soldiers pass my window and go to Bishop Norman's. After a while Bishop Norman came to me and told me, 'Those military men want you.' Obviously I suspected that a difficult situation was happening as the three soldiers had come heavily armed with grenades, guns and the like, so I knew exactly who they were looking for.

When I went to Bishop Norman's they told me immediately, 'We have come for you.' I said, 'Why?' and they replied, 'We want to interview you.' So I said, 'Okay, I'm ready,' but they then said, 'No, we are not interviewing you here, we want take you to Gikongoro for questioning, we have to take you there.' I knew it was not for questioning that they were taking me but for killing, that was very clear. I said, 'If you want papers or whatever, they can be found and provided here because...' They interrupted, 'You man, you seem to be joking, you don't know what is happening. You're wasting our time. We want to take you away. Enough is enough, no more arguments, we have to go.'

I realised that there was no point in wasting time and knew they would drop me at the nearest roadblock and then the militia would cut me in pieces, so I made two requests. 'Could you allow me to say something to Norman.' And they replied, 'Yes, provided you don't move out of this house.' My second request was, 'I'll have to say goodbye to my wife who is just next door.' They said, 'Fine.' I knew then that the matter was very serious because it was clear I had now been arrested. So we went inside the house, actually into their bedroom because that was the only private place. The image I recall from that room will never, never leave me, as it was a real example of God loving people in a time of many difficulties. Madelene, Norman's wife, who has now gone to heaven, had been following the discussion with the soldiers and was there on her knees, praying. She knew that it was now all over for us, that we had no chance of surviving, so she went into their room and we found her on her knees. I assumed she was praying for us so we didn't bother her. She continued with her job and whatever I told Norman, she heard as well.

I spoke to Norman about three things. 'I think you can see what is happening,' I said and he replied, 'Yes, I can see, I understand,' meaning it was clear they were going kill me, it was all over for us. I want to emphasise this point because people tend to think that during the genocide every Muhutu went about killing every Mututsi. But that is very wrong. If it was only ethnicity, then Madelene should have betrayed us. Instead she shut herself away in their room and here she was, praying for us with all her heart. We only happened to see her because we broke in to their room so I could talk with Norman alone.

Next I told Norman in what drawer I had put my will, as I had already written it. Believe me, it had not been an easy thing to write my will when less than forty years old. Imagine sitting down and saying to God, 'You have given me enough time to write my will, so let me write it now because I know I will soon be going to heaven. Why should I leave my things scattered about behind me?' So I was able to tell Norman, 'Now about my vehicle, if you discover any relative of mine has survived, give it to him or her. If not, then it can go to the Church.' And I made arrangements for the disposal of various things and how they should be used. Even though it had not been easy to write I had done it, all the time thinking about how terrible it was, yet at the same time saying, 'Thank you God for giving me these few extra years.' It was really terrible.

Then I told him the third thing. 'Norman, I have served the Church faithfully. We have prayed together, so have the courage to claim my dead body and bury it because it would be a shame for it to be eaten by dogs. I know it will be very difficult for you but please have the courage to claim my body and bury me.' He could not speak but I saw him nod his head meaning, 'Yes I will do it.'

I had only been given a few minutes alone with Norman so I moved out of the room and the soldiers took me outside. Before Norman and I entered the bedroom they blocked the two doors to make sure I didn't run away, but there was no possibility of this happening for if there had been, I would have done this long before their arrival.

This occurred towards the end of May, and I had been waiting there for death for about two months.

When we reached the front of the house I was staying in, which as I said before was adjacent to Norman's house, I asked again if I could say goodbye to my wife and children. They told me to do it quickly, as there was no time to waste. When I wanted to put on my clerical shirt they said, 'No, no, no, we don't want to waste any more time.' And I remember my wife saying to them, 'Why don't you take us as well, because we know you are going to kill him. Why don't you kill us together? Why do you want to kill us separately?' They simply told her, 'We shall come back for you. We are taking him now but never you mind, we shall come back very soon for you and the children.'

So they put me in a vehicle but the vehicle wouldn't start. They kept trying to start it but the vehicle simply refused to go. They then said, 'Give us your money.' I looked at them and laughed and then took my wallet from my pocket and handed it over to them saying, 'I don't have any rights over my body any more, because if I had any rights I would say, "No". But now you are asking me for whatever money I have, it's no longer mine. If you can take me you can take my money, that's not a problem.' They then looked into my wallet – I think there was less than ten dollars there, the only remaining money I had to feed and keep the whole family. They just looked at it and gave it back to me and said, 'This isn't money we are talking about.' So I put it back in my pocket.

We got in the car with one soldier sitting beside me, another behind me, and another at the steering wheel. They started up the engine and it kept roaring, roaring, roaring. After couple of minutes of this they seemed a bit confused, as the vehicle wasn't moving for reasons I couldn't understand. They then looked at each other, then at me, and ordered me to 'Get out. We'll come back for you.'

I got out and they drove off without beating me up, abusing or insulting me, apart from using harsh language. They had come for me but left without me and never returned, even though I had nothing or no one to count on but the grace of God.

Imminent danger

During all of May our belongings remained in our former house along the road running between the hospital and the church and Diocesan offices. Although we had shifted to the school we didn't take our belongings. Meals were prepared there but sometimes I would go back to the house to take a bath or something. I went there regularly almost twice a day. When the militia discovered I was going there regularly, they organised themselves to wait for me there and to catch and kill me there, then they would just finish up and vanish. They enjoyed killings of that nature, just going off and torturing or killing somebody, then after finishing, leaving to do something else. I was inside the house and felt as if a voice was telling me, 'Alex, you are in danger.' I looked around but there was no one in the house. Very quickly, I moved out and when I reached the gate, I saw somebody spying on me from the hospital, so I moved quickly away from the gate and started towards the school. As I was reaching there, I saw a group of youths coming down, so immediately took a short cut. When they saw me they stopped, then started laughing and began walking back. I quickly walked back to the house from where I had come and saw they had turned back. From the way they were laughing and the like, I could tell that they were saying to me, 'We were coming to punish you, just because you kept moving around the place, but you were too clever, so we shall have to kill you another day.' Their behaviour was strange, with them often moving around in big groups, attacking people after sessions of heavy drinking and smoking. Sometimes they acted under the orders of leaders, carrying out fierce attacks where they killed each and every person they found, destroying everything. At other times they attacked in small groups, raping and torturing, but sometimes they just seemed too tired, and so would postpone the killings.

I cannot forget this day. Here I was in my house as usual, but on this day, when danger approached, God said, 'Alex, you're in danger.' He told me this at just the right time, because within three minutes, it would have been too late and they would have caught me in the house, killed me there and finished me off. It was a very significant thing the way God kept protecting us in very, very, many ways. When God tells you danger is coming, you can feel it; you can really hear him. God speaks and we are able to hear his voice, not only when he is guiding us in the path of righteousness but also when he is warning us of danger.

Sticking together

People kept passing by, running away from Kigali. Knowing we had no chance of surviving, they kept offering to take our children, our two eldest daughters, so that they at least would survive. We had been thinking about sending them to their aunt in Kenya or to some other relatives and were tempted over and over again to send them away with others so that they at least could escape. Some other people offered to take the two youngest children, because children, having no identity cards could very easily escape the roadblocks. But whenever we prayed, we felt that God was not permitting us to separate the family. We felt that if we sent our children away and they died along the way and we happened to survive, we would have guilty consciences because we had given them away to death. Some Bahutu families wanted to keep our youngest boy, who was by then less than two years old, by pretending he was their child or grandchild, so as to at least save him, because for us dying was no longer a possibility but a reality.

We felt God was telling us, 'Stick together, stay together.' So this is what we did.

CHAPTER FIVE

Saved for what purpose?

After the three soldiers had gone, it seemed even the soldiers were now becoming involved, wanting to do the job themselves because they felt the militia was not doing its dirty work well enough. I felt that we had to attempt to run away but again we thought that it was imperative to pray, to know exactly what was God's will. I said to my wife, 'Why don't we pray to find out if it really is God's will for us to try to run away?' because the question of surviving there in Kigeme was now impossible. So in the month of May we prayed and asked for a sign from God. I said, 'What sign will we ask God to give us?' for if we wanted to escape we needed to take the road to Burundi, to where the nearest border point was, a distance of 40 kilometres, or a little less at some points.

So my wife said, 'We need to send somebody to find out whether it is a safe way out for us. Can we ask for a sign that if the person we send comes back and tells us that there are no roadblocks, then it is safe?' Now from where we were we could see the first roadblock so I replied, 'How can you ask that for a sign when you already know the roadblocks are there?' But then I felt sorry and said, 'I have to repent because if God wants us to go, he can take the roadblocks away.' So, we prayed there, then sent one of the pastors, Samuel. This pastor was himself a Muhutu and not a killer. He was very sympathetic to us, and talked and prayed with us. So again I must emphasise that not all the Bahutu betrayed us, because when you love God and you love Jesus, you will remain faithful to them even during turmoil.

So Samuel took the car and drove all the way to the Burundi border. When he came back he told us that there were roadblocks everywhere and the militia were searching everything, even beneath vehicles. They were so thorough that you couldn't hide a single thing, let alone a human being in them. Yet one month later, as will be seen later, the sign we were asking for was given.

In a military barracks

One evening, Bishop Norman knocked on my door and I opened it to him. He was immersed in deep reflection and after a time told me, 'Bishop Alex, I have been informed today that the soldiers are coming here.' Then I asked Bishop Norman if he had told them about our presence or was there some other plan. He told me that he had informed their leaders about us and there was no other plan, apart from trusting in the Lord.

The secondary school was to become a military school for training officers. They had been in Kigali but as the war approached they moved to the next spot towards the south, to a place called Nyanza, and then to another as the war came nearer again. As the Rwandan Patriotic Army came in from Uganda, the Government Army retreated before it. The Government Army now needed many more officers so they were training them in a crash program. They numbered roughly a thousand, which was why they needed to occupy the secondary school, moving in with their trainers, bosses and the like.

So we stayed there in an army barracks for one whole month, waiting upon the Almighty to protect us. It was very strange, as I could not imagine myself surviving in an army barracks, among the very army organising and carrying out the systematic killing of Batutsi. It was as if God wanted to show us that 'I can protect you anywhere, anyhow and against anybody.'

But I knew then that it was over for us and said, 'We are going to be in an army barracks. How can we survive in an army barracks?' Yet it seems as if God was bringing them there to protect us. We stayed inside the house, locking ourselves in and saying, 'Okay let us at least spend the last few hours together with the family,' for we knew that as soon as the army arrived here they would kill us before doing anything else. What else could the army do? How could they keep the enemy in their backyard, for to them, all Batutsi were enemies, and so must be killed?

So they came. When they arrived at the door you can imagine how we felt immediately on hearing the first knock, for when soldiers knock, they have a particular knock, a really hard knock. Our hearts jumped. Obviously I went to open the door, because if I didn't, the door would have been blown to pieces. When I opened the door, I found a tall lady there, an army major, and this lady knew me. She just happened to be an Anglican who had studied with my wife in secondary education. She said to me, 'Hi, Bishop' and to my wife, 'Hi, Grace.' I said 'Hi,' And she replied, 'Hi. Are you still alive?' I said 'Yes, through God's grace we are still alive.' I then ventured to test the ground to see how things were. I said, 'But Jeanne' (that was her name; I didn't say Major or whatever), I said, 'Jeanne, I hope you are going to kill us in a better way. Just shoot us with your guns, because we don't want to be chopped into pieces with machetes.' Her reply was very interesting, indeed prophetic, remembering that she was the Number Two commander of this school, under the Colonel. I wonder if today she even remembers her words, but this is what she said:

'Bishop, we are not killers. God has brought us here and we shall protect you.'

Those words have never left me. She became very friendly. When a major becomes friendly with you when up till then even the simplest soldier has threatened you, it is hard to imagine what you should do in the situation. We did not even have a right to a decent death, let alone the right to live. Then suddenly the situation changes and a senior army officer is being friendly to you. Those three soldiers who nearly killed us were at most sergeants, and we had been at the mercy of the militia, where any young man could have killed us and got away with it or even been rewarded for it.

It was amazing. This major even occupied the house adjacent to ours, as by then Bishop Norman had moved to another house and we had moved into a smaller one. We started a different life altogether because we were now in an army barracks and therefore the militia no longer had access to us. No person from outside could enter there without the permission of the army.

A visit from the Colonel

A few days later, somebody, I think a captain, came to me to say that in a few minutes, the commander, the

Colonel, would be visiting us. I was so surprised. You might have told me that an angel from heaven was coming to visit us. I couldn't believe my ears – such an important man with so many powers, who had the right to kill us or to protect us, at least for the moment. Even when he had been visiting us for twenty or thirty minutes, I still couldn't believe it. We didn't know each other, although I had heard of his name but not much else about him. He came along and greeted me, then asked, 'How are you?' I said, 'We are fine.' We didn't talk about anything serious, although to me he appeared to be a serious and thoughtful man. But deep down in my heart I must confess that I did not fully trust him or rather any of them. Then he said to me, 'Why are you locking the children in? They have a right to go out in the sun. We are not killers. We shall protect you.'

And in fact they did protect us, although I suspect that among those teachers still there that some who had been dismissed or were to be transferred may have wanted to kill us. I can't be sure, because when you are dealing with soldiers you sometimes have to guess certain things about their motives because they won't tell you exactly why they are attempting to do this or that. One day I ventured to ask this major, 'Now, you may not be intending to kill us but what if some of your people come at night and kill us. How will you know?' And then she told me 'We know our people. We know how to handle security within our area and within our camp. So don't worry. We shall protect you.' So when I heard this, I suspected that there were some bad elements there who were probably planning to kill us. So we stayed there in the barracks and some serious threats to us still occurred during that time.

More danger

Sometime in the middle or second half of June three Roman Catholic Bishops were killed, I understand by a soldier who was supposed to be guarding them. At that time, the Rwandan Patriotic Front was conquering town after town and had captured the place where the Bishops were living. When I heard the announcement of their deaths on the radio, I knew that without doubt I would now be killed in revenge for their deaths. Various messages had been transmitted to me with this just threat, each saying that if any of the Hutu Bishops were killed, then they would kill me as well.

Despite the fact that we were in an army barracks, the militia and the political leaders of the area were so angry about this that they said they would not rest until they had our heads. The militia made several threats and attempts to get the army to hand us over and kept insisting, 'Give us Bishop Alex and his wife and children. We want to kill them.' The army said, 'No way,' so the militia tried to break in. The army said, 'We are the force in charge of their protection and if any of you attempts to enter our camp, we shall shoot you.' The threats became so great that at one stage, the militia threatened to take Bishop Norman and his wife as hostages – if we were not handed over to the militia, then Bishop Norman and his wife would be killed. Fortunately the threats were not carried out but there is no doubt that if we had not been in an army barracks, we would have been killed there and then. The militia would have come and killed us immediately in revenge.

When the then Minister of Defence who was also the Commander of the military visited this army barracks and learnt that I was still alive he was so angry. 'How come this fellow is still alive? What have you been doing? Why didn't you kill him? He has seen so much that he has to die.' In the meantime we had sent a message to him, wanting him to help us and give us continued protection and this made him even angrier. A soldier who was an escort for this Commander was a Batutsi although they didn't know this, and he heard the Commander speaking angrily, 'This man should die because he has seen so much. He is still alive, he should be killed.' So this young man came back and told me, 'Bishop Alex I don't think you have long to live'. I said, 'Why?' and he replied, 'Our boss has said that you have to be killed because you have seen so much. He wonders how come you are still alive.'

The helicopter

Within two days or so, a clear message from the Commander was sent saying that a helicopter was coming to take Bishop Alex and his wife and his family to the north. So the helicopter came and landed some 50 metres from the house where we were staying. Obviously, the pilot had to report to the commander of the barracks, the Colonel. The pilot told him that he had come to fetch Bishop Alex and his family and then the Colonel asked him, 'And where are you taking him?' When he replied, 'To Gisenyi' (that is in the northern part of the country), the Colonel inquired no more because he knew exactly what was taking place. So he told the pilot, 'I'm ordering you to fly off immediately. Leave my camp before I deal with you!' For the pilot this was suicide because it meant disobeying his boss, the Commander. This happened towards the end of June and things were getting hotter and hotter.

After that, the Colonel sent a message to me and said, 'Bishop Alex, you saw the helicopter which landed just near to your house?' I said, 'Yes, I saw it.' 'It was coming for you, but I judged it better to send it back. I'll tell you more.' So next day he came and told me personally, 'Bishop Alex, that helicopter was sent by our boss and it was coming to take you to Gisenyi, that is the north, to the army barracks there. And I think you understand the rest.' I told him I understood. He then told me, 'I sent it away and you understand the consequences.' I replied, 'Yes, I understand.'

So, he was in a way starting to distance himself from the leadership of the army as things were getting more and more tense. Fortunately, at the very time the helicopter was sent back, the Commander was on a mission in the Congo, so he couldn't deal with the matter immediately. It was becoming clearer and clearer that the RPF were going to be victorious because they were getting closer and closer to Kigali, so things were getting tougher and tougher for the government army. The RPF had already captured a big chunk of the country and everybody was becoming conscious that there would be consequences for those who had taken part in the killing.

I can remember the Colonel saying, 'Why didn't they kill you before I came here? If you are killed now, your blood will be on my head, so why didn't they kill you before I came? You were alive when I came so why do they want to kill you while I'm here? Now I have to make up my mind as a grown man and decide what precautions I need to take.'

The French Army arrives

Just as the RPF was beginning to take over the country, the French Army suddenly arrived in this part of Rwanda. People were jubilant, happy and excited. I could see across the hills and saw flags and people carrying flowers. I asked somebody, 'Now what's happening?' They said, 'The French are coming, the French are coming to rescue us. The French are coming to protect us.' Then towards the end of July, with news that the RPF was coming, people became terribly afraid. Soldiers were running away, and all of a sudden I found the mood changing. Then I saw some jeeps. I had been listening to the radio and it was saying that the French were coming on a rescue mission to protect people and the like. But it was very clear the French were coming not to protect people, but to fight back the RPF soldiers and stop them, because when you come to protect people, you don't come with guns and jeeps.

The Colonel takes precautions

From the window of the house I was staying in, I saw fifty jeeps and helicopters passing, as well as armed vehicles with heavy weapons. And as they passed I heard what they were saying – they were coming to see whether there were any people still alive whom they could rescue. 'Okay,' I said, 'Good. Let me send somebody to them.' Then the army Colonel came to me and said, 'I think I need to take precautions and keep on protecting you. The French people have the means of helping to rescue you so let's approach them to see if they can take you across to Bukavu or whatever.' So he sent a message to them although I did not believe him. All along I hadn't really trusted him and felt that at some stage he would kill me. I believed I was being held as a hostage tool, to be used in negotiations of some kind.

So until the last minute, when I discovered that he really meant it, I felt a sense of insecurity and did not really trust him. He sent a message and also a pastor, the Diocesan Secretary. I requested the pastor to go and see the French and to tell them a Bishop was awaiting death there, and now that they were here, could they help me and my wife and children. When the two messengers came back and said that the French did not think this was very urgent now, my big question was, 'Well what was urgent for them?' If rescuing people was not urgent then it was clear what was urgent for them was to fight back the RPF soldiers. This raised questions for our safety.

The Colonel came back to me and said, 'Now, Alex, what do we do? I need to take precautions because things are moving from bad to worse here and I may run into troubles myself. So you should either remain here and we go, or we help you out of the country. It is up to you to choose.' In my mind I was thinking, 'From here to where we want to go in the Congo is around some 30, if not 40 kilometres. To get there you have to cross about thirty natural forests so probably this man will take me, kill me and throw me away there.' But then I said to myself, 'It's better to risk this than staying here', for by this time, Kigali and Butare had been captured. The Colonel then said, 'I will be back so get ready to depart.'

Escape to the border

At exactly one o'clock, the Colonel's personal vehicle arrived and he was inside. We sat behind him, my wife on one side, myself on the other, with our four children in between. Behind us were three heavily armed soldiers and in front, a jeep full of heavily armed soldiers. He then told them to go ahead and remove all the roadblocks.

So I left Kigeme at one o'clock, when everybody could see us. People from around there saw us passing and I waved to them. They said, 'The Bishop is going, the Bishop is going.' The militia could see me too, but did not know exactly where I was going. We drove for one and half to two hours before reaching the border of the Congo and Rwanda. Now the big problem was how we would cross the border, as the Colonel told us, 'I cannot cross as a soldier in uniform because it will be considered aggression. So I can't take you out of the country.' Although it was only 50 metres across, crossing the border was impossible for us. The militia was roaming around so we could still be killed there and chopped into pieces, even at the bridge.

Now the Colonel asked me, 'Do you have passports?' I said 'Yes, I have them.' 'For yourself and your wife?' I said, 'Yes, we have them.' So he gave them to a soldier who took them to customs. They were then stamped and brought back to us. Then the Colonel called over one of the customs officers and said, 'Why am I being kept standing here? Take these people across, put them in the Congo, then come back to me while I am here,' for he could see what would happen. We then entered a different vehicle and just when were expecting to find ourselves in heaven, we found ourselves in the Congo, not dead, but alive – Bishop Alex, his wife and four children, two girls and two boys. Nobody ever harmed us. No one insulted us. No one abused us. For three months we had been kept safe in God's hands.

A refugee again

And I remember at the customs office across the river, the Congolese customs man asking me, 'Are you from Rwanda?' I said 'Yes.' Then he said, 'Are you not a Tutsi?' I said, 'I don't know, but I have been told this over and over again.' And then he went on and asked me, 'How come that you are alive?' I told him, 'I don't know.' Then he asked me, 'Do I register you as a refugee or what?' I said 'You can write whatever you want. I don't know.' 'I don't understand', he said. I told him, 'I don't understand either.' He said 'What do I write?' I said 'You write whatever you like because I do not know what I am. My passport has been stamped. I am here. I don't know where I am going. I don't know why I am coming here. I don't understand.' He said 'I don't understand either.'

Now we said, 'God obviously does not want us to leave this earth yet so we should calm down,' so we thought back on our journey. When we left, there was not a single roadblock on the way. A military escort took us and another vehicle went ahead of us saying, 'There is a car coming. Take off all the roadblocks.' And all the roadblocks were taken away. Whenever we passed, there was no roadblock. And only when we reached Zaire, when we went across into the Congo, did we realise, 'Goodness, we didn't find one single roadblock along the way.' God had waited for a whole month to give us this sign. When we finally moved out, we had no idea that the roadblocks were going to be taken away for us, yet along the way we found there were no roadblocks. This sign, given a month after we had prayed for it, was a clear sign that this was God's time for us to move out.

Our own vehicle had been sent ahead from Kigeme so we were able to drive all the way to Bukavu. Here I was again, starting a new life as a refugee.

Saved for what purpose?

Anyone hearing of or reading this story might ask, 'Why have you Alex, been spared? You would not be the first to ask this question – I was probably the first ask it and it was a big question. 'Why am I alive? Why am I not dead, because all the others have been killed?' And I definitely knew that the answer was not because I was really righteous as I knew a number of righteous people who had been killed, people who were really godly and righteous. So the question of being righteous was out of question.

And it was not because I was a Bishop, because with only one Bishop dead among nine Bishops, life could go on without any problem. Furthermore, if only three Bishops remained they could still consecrate others. That was another question less. Anyway, it wasn't as if I was sitting in a position someone else wanted. So why was I alive?

Slowly I began to feel that God had a purpose for me because God had performed all these miracles, saving me from all sorts of troubles over three months, not once or twice or three times, but nearly every other day. Hardly a day went by when God had to do something to protect me. And when I look back, I can see that each of the miracles was different from the others, from people disagreeing among themselves, soldiers being unable to take me away even when I was put in their jeep, the helicopter which had come purposely to take me being chased away. Whoever doesn't believe in miracles will have to explain to me how else these things came about. It seems to me that God kept changing methods as if to prove to me that he could rescue from any angle, from anywhere, using anything he liked, no matter what the danger.

But I still had a big question mark over what was God's purpose in this? I need to tell you where I was when I began to ask this question. In 1984, I had gone to Bukavu to spend six months in that Diocese to do a course in rural development. In that time I also organised bible school studies, bible groups and prayer groups. I also requested the Bishop of Bukavu to show me a place where I could help in evangelisation.

Reports of my death

Now the people who had been working with me back in 1984 loved me very much and had been praying for me recently, especially when they heard that an English newspaper had reported my death after the story went around that an Assistant Bishop had been killed during the turmoils. But when they saw me they told me, 'Bishop Alex, even when we learnt that you were dead we did not believe it. We kept on praying for you.' It's amazing how you can continue to believe when people who seem to be knowledgeable tell you things contrary to what you want to hear. So they didn't believe it and said, 'No, we'll keep on praying for him.' When they saw me, they were so happy and they gave us a nice house, fed us, cooked for us and visited us. They even brought us money. And would you believe that when I crossed the border, I had just run out of money.

Going back to the whole question of money, I found God's provision so miraculous. When the whole thing started and the killings began, I gave someone a cheque and sent them to the bank to withdraw all the money I had in my account. Just one day later the bank was closed and people were no longer allowed to withdraw money. So throughout the troubles I had money to use and didn't lack anything. And when I did run out of money was at the very time I crossed the border. Money now started pouring in. People kept coming with money, clothes and all sorts of things. Within a few days, I was already alongside the Bishop of Bukavu in the hills, doing confirmations.

Temptation

But still the big question in my mind was, 'Why am I alive?'

Another phenomenon occurred. Friends from abroad also learnt that I had managed to cross to the Congo and were saying, 'Bishop Alex how can we help you, what can we do for you?' When somebody – I think Tearfund – offered to give me a scholarship to get away from it all, it was a great temptation to leave, especially to forget about it all and to try to get over the trauma and the like.

It was a very great temptation. But a voice always told me – 'Bishop Alex, if God has spared you, you know that to take away your wife and four children to a nice place and forget about it all – surely that would be a miscalculation on the side of God.' So I told these people, that even though I felt so exhausted and so broken, I needed to pray more to know exactly why it was that God had spared my life.

Flight to Kenya

I was praying and asking God's will and thinking about how God's miracles had accompanied me along the way. We crossed the border on the fourth of July, two weeks after the flood of people from Rwanda, soldiers, people, everybody, started crowding into Bukavu, militia included. It was not safe for us to stay there so we decided it would be good for us to go to Nairobi to where we could pray quietly and ask God for his guidance to know exactly what we should be doing.

We went and booked a flight on a small plane but the company required a bond of $US1500 as a guarantee in case we were expelled and they had to take us back to where we had come from. Because I didn't have the money, they said that they would look for other people to take our places. I said, 'Don't write me off. Tomorrow I will have the money.' They said 'We're not joking. We're serious.' I said, 'I don't have the money but God will provide. Tomorrow we shall fly together'. Something cropped up and the plane did not depart that day. Then in a miraculous way, the following day I had the $1500 and said to the airline people, 'Here is the money.' They said, 'You have it?' I said, 'Here's the money.' They said, 'Unbelievable.' I said, 'I am used to this. This is not new. God works in a very miraculous way – providing money, preserving lives, doing this and that.'

I can still remember this pilot, for when we reached Entebbe in Uganda on the way to Nairobi, he wanted to have a photo taken of him with our whole family. He was really happy and said, 'I just can't understand how you can say "I'm going to have the money", and within a few hours you have the exact money, no more, no less.' That was true for the money we received was exactly the $1500 needed as a bond to get to Kenya.

Father to the fatherless

So we went to Kenya and when we arrived we prayed and the voice of God came to us very clearly that now we were to become the father of the fatherless and that we had to care for the orphans. It was very clear that God had not preserved us simply because we were righteous, God had not preserved us because he wanted us to go away to some nice corner of the world to just forget about it all. God wanted us to go back to Rwanda, to where there were now thousands and thousands of orphans, and we were to care for them. Although the message was very clear, the means by which this would be done I had still to find out along the way. But for now, whenever anybody asked me, 'Why have you survived?' I replied, 'Because God wants me to take care of the orphans.' The matter of whether to go away with my wife and children was ruled out.

That was in July, and as early as August, I was back in Rwanda caring for the orphans, carrying out the mission to which the Lord had entrusted me. I had learned afresh that God can speak and if you are attentive you are able to hear him. He can move you, he can shake you, but God has many ways of protecting us.

Justice and reconciliation is not only a Christian imperative but is a must for every person in their right mind, whoever thinks and loves life. We must work towards this because we cannot go on and on as we have. I cannot continue to live in this vicious circle of violence, whereby I became a refugee as a child, then as a young man and then again as an adult when we had to

Children playing, acting out death by machete

take our children out with us. It only remains to be taken
out with our grandchildren and by then, I should be too
weak and not able to walk. It is too terrible to even think
about it. I have become committed to reconciliation not
only because I have had to live with reconciliation
through this circle of violence but so too have many other
people who also have experienced the same problems as
myself. I feel that any sensible, sensitive Rwandese who
thinks things through in a clear-minded way, should work
towards peace and reconciliation and make a real
commitment towards it. They should commit themselves
to that because we cannot go on as we have done for

over forty years. Almost everyone has become a refugee in one way or another.

It is my hope that this feeling is shared by many Rwandese, and that together we can work towards a much more just and peaceful country.

Some Rwandese and even some outsiders may have different opinions. These people may still delight in the polarisation of the Rwandese, seeing things in ethnic colours, and knowingly or unknowingly still sowing the seeds of hatred. The Rwandese holding such views will be people who associated with those who planned or implemented the genocide. Indeed they may be either afraid of being judged or else ashamed of what they have stood for in the past. Most will have good jobs and a lot of money and whatever they do or say, will try to justify themselves. And those from outside the country (and they do exist) who hold similar views, are simply misguided or wrongly informed about affairs concerning Rwanda.

Epilogue
Alan Nichols –
The Barakabaho Foundation

In 1994 when Rwanda and the surrounding refugee camps were filled with fear and hopelessness, one man at the top of the 'death lists', who had been rescued from the genocide, had a vision to become 'father to the fatherless.' Beginning as an idea only, it was my privilege to be the first foreigner to hear about the vision. Something in me responded, perhaps because of my own background as head of a child welfare agency in the 1980s, for I immediately believed and trusted him. That trust has never been undermined, despite the fearful business of a country recovering from genocide, much trauma still to be dealt with as victims continue to live alongside perpetrators, and a thousand other difficulties almost impossible to imagine in a country as peaceful and prosperous as Australia.

In the year 2001, the Barakabaho Foundation is a thriving national child welfare organisation operating along thoroughly professional lines. It has placed 8000 war orphans with foster families and has over seven years given them continuous support. First it handed out basic supplies and food from the immense relief funds which poured into Rwanda in the year following the genocide. Then it provided access for the children to education, social supports, health care, and then support in trauma counselling and reconciliation. The agency has become so successful and professional that the Rwandan Government now regards it as the 'national model' of child care. Other agencies, and even international non-government organisations, are sent to Barakabaho to see how it is done.

Drawings used in trauma counselling for genocide victims

After a few years had passed following the genocide, the main energy switched from placing children with foster families, to the wider social problems of the country. A women's department was commenced, which is providing significant training and support for women now heading households, enabling those women whose husbands were killed in the genocide to become the breadwinners.

Barakabaho has started its own reconciliation workshops across the country and this has led to the

Trauma counselling now covers other disasters such as road accidents and landslides

development of trauma counselling, a service quite unknown to the country before. There is now an association of thirty-eight professional trauma counsellors with a central office and counselling centre in Kigali, funded by Trocaire, an Irish agency. This group is doing amazing work right across the country, introducing something quite alien to Central African culture. It has now switched from counselling people about the hidden traumas of the genocide and moved into counselling about HIV and AIDS. This is an emerging health problem of Rwanda as in other parts of Africa. It has been compounded in Rwanda by the imbalance of men and women within the Tutsi subculture and by the enormous dislocation of the young men who joined the militia and engaged in the genocide. These young men fled for their lives into neighbouring countries and then returned. Because of the breakdown of social inhibitions and taboos, armies on the move always accelerate AIDS. Prior to the genocide there were strong taboos within Rwandan culture – both Hutu and Tutsi – with regard to sexual activity outside marriage, and promiscuity within it.

As for Bishop Alexis, he moved on as a result of being consecrated a Diocesan Bishop in 1997. He is now the Chairman of the National Board of Barakabaho rather than its Executive Director. As a consequence, Barakabaho has been learning to move from being an informal organisation founded and directed by a charismatic personality, towards becoming a professional organisation with its own mission statement, line management, and various accountabilities to beneficiaries, local communities, regional committees and a national board. This transition has been supported by AngliCORD as its main overseas funding support, and with funds from AusAid.

Very early on, Bishop Alexis was appointed by the Rwandan Government to be a member of the Board of the National Fund for the Survivors of Genocide. Based in Kigali, this fund seeks and attracts some international funding. These funds are being distributed by way of compensation to the families of genocide victims. The Board is also the channel for any international funding from overseas governments or the United Nations for the process of transporting prisoners to the location of their crimes where they are facing local village courts. During 2000 and 2001, it will process the 70,000 people in jail awaiting trial for involvement in some aspect of the genocide.

Gahini is the centre of Bishop Alexis' new Diocese. There he has made new appointments for Diocesan administration and leadership and established mission priorities. He has himself taken a lead in direct evangelisation, preaching publicly in market places across the prefecture of Umutare, which is precisely the same territory as covered by the Diocese of Gahini.

He has also dreamed up the idea of an income-generation project of substantial size, along the banks of Lake Muhazi and had it up and running within one year of its conception. He calls this project the 'seeds of peace'. It already has a tourist picnic park, a 'milk house' where traditional Rwandan yogurt is served, a 'king's house' which reproduces the way the ancient kings of Rwanda used to live, and a restaurant serving chicken and goat. From the slowly emerging profits of this enterprise, three thatched houses are gradually being built, each with their own bathrooms and kitchens and facing one of the most beautiful lake vistas in the world. These will be available for hire by ambassadors, foreigners and the emerging middle class of Rwanda for holiday breaks or an overnight stay on the way north to the Akagera National Park. Already this project is self-

Tourist Park in Gahini, an income generation project

supporting and putting small profits into the building of the thatched lodges. The plan is that within a year, this project will contribute towards the cost of building a ministry training centre alongside it.

Bishop Alex has a five year plan for the future of the Diocese, training new clergy, sending promising clergy overseas for further training, evangelising uneducated people in the bush, assisting catechists to explore faith with new people and lead them to baptism and confirmation. These are church processes towards a much more significant goal: to create faith communities in the part of Rwanda most hurt by the genocide, so that forgiveness and reconciliation can happen, and so that a similar genocide never occurs again. He wants his country healed, and believes Jesus Christ is the key to that healing.

Bishop Alexis

angels